Survival Skills

Tony Norman

GARETH**STEVENS**
PUBLISHING
A Member of the WRC Media Family of Companies

Please visit our web site at: www.garethstevens.com
For a free color catalog describing Gareth Stevens Publishing's
list of high-quality books and multimedia programs, call
1-800-542-2595 (USA) or 1-800-387-3178 (Canada).
Gareth Stevens Publishing's fax: (414) 332-3567.

Library of Congress Cataloging-in-Publication Data

Norman, Tony.
  Survival skills / Tony Norman.
    p. cm. — (Action sports)
  ISBN 0-8368-6370-4 (lib. bdg.)
  1. Survival skills. I. Title. II. Action sports (Milwaukee, Wis.)
  GF86.N67 2006
  613.6'9—dc22   2005054181

This edition first published in 2006 by
Gareth Stevens Publishing
A Member of the WRC Media Family of Companies
330 West Olive Street, Suite 100
Milwaukee, Wisconsin 53212 USA

This U.S. edition copyright © 2006 by Gareth Stevens, Inc. Original
edition copyright © 2006 by ticktock Entertainment Ltd. First published in
2006 by ticktock Media Ltd., Unit 2, Orchard Business Centre, North Farm Road,
Tunbridge Wells, Kent TN2 3XF, U.K.

Gareth Stevens editor: Carol Ryback
Gareth Stevens designer: Scott M. Krall

The author would like to thank Patrick McGlinchey, from the Backwoods Survival
School in Scotland.

The publishers would like to thank Natural Pathways Survival Company for their
help in making this book.

Photo credits: (t)=top; (b)=bottom
CORBIS: / Tim McGuire 13(t). Mike Forti: 15(b), 17(b).
Natural Pathways Survival Company: / Hannah Nicholls 17(t).
Free Nature Pictures: 20(b).
Alamy: / Dynamic Graphics Group / IT Stock Free 24–25.

Every effort has been made to trace the copyright holders, and we apologize
in advance for any unintentional omissions. We will be pleased to insert the
appropriate acknowledgments in any subsequent edition of this publication.

Printed in the United States of America

1 2 3 4 5 6 7 8 9 10 09 08 07 06

Contents

On the Edge   4–5

Day Tripping   6–7

Navigation   8–9

What to Wear   10–11

Food and Drink   12–13

Emergency!   14–15

Gimme Shelter   16–17

Campfires   18–19

Drinking in the Wild   20–21

Finding Food   22–23

Signaling for Help   24–25

Brain Power   26–27

Types of Wilderness   28–29

Glossary   30–31

Index   32

On the Edge

Most people like to stay comfortable. They do the same things, in the same places, with the same people, every day. Others want to get outside and explore the natural world. Hiking through a wild area is a great way to get away, as long as the hikers are prepared.

A hike is a long walk in the countryside. Hikers enjoy the scenery, fresh air, and exercise.

Going hiking

Something as simple as going for a walk in the woods can be risky for people who are not properly prepared. Hikers must know what to do if the weather conditions change and how to respond if they become injured or lost.

Survival skills

It is not unusual for lost hikers to spend the night outdoors. Basic survival skills and common sense save lives. Such information is useful not only for hikers, but also for active people who spend a lot of time outdoors. Simple survival skills are as essential as having the proper clothing, food, and equipment. This knowledge may come in handy in other emergency situations, such as in case of a remote plane crash.

Survival facts - Did you know?

Swiss Army knives come in many varieties and, in addition to their knife blades, often include features such as a can opener, screwdriver, scissors, and a toothpick. The newest models may also indicate altitude (height) and temperature.

Fire

Water

Food

Signals

A mirror can catch the sunlight to signal rescuers.

Relaxing in the wilderness is a fulfilling experience.

Day Tripping

Hiking is usually more enjoyable when done with a partner or as part of a group. Hikers should always tell someone where they are going and what time they plan on returning. That way, a rescue team knows where to start searching if problems arise.

Preparing for the hike

Hikers do not need much equipment for a one-day hike. The best items to carry include a map, compass, pocket knife, water, and food. Hikers should always use sunscreen and may need insect repellent. Good hiking boots and layers of clothing help keep hikers comfortable.

Preparing for survival

Hikers should always take a simple survival kit along, just in case of problems. The kit needs to contain basic equipment, such as a lighter or matches, a small, tough plastic bag, and a whistle, glass mirror, or even a bright bandana — all of which come in handy for signaling for help. Other useful items include strong waxed thread, safety pins, a flashlight, and first-aid kit with sterile wipes, band-aids, and cold packs.

Mountain climbers use special gear and must learn cold-weather survival techniques.

Survival facts - Did you know?

Rescuers need to know a person's name and whom to contact in an emergency. Always carry identification.

Nobody ever expects to get lost. Hikers should always carry a basic survival kit with them.

TRUE STORIES
The 1972 Andes Mountains plane crash remains one of the most infamous survival experiences of modern times. Survivors had no choice but to eat the bodies of the other victims — or die.

A first-aid kit should include sterile wipes, band-aids, and cold packs.

Chocolate is a good high-energy snack, but keep it cool - or it melts!

Sunscreen protects against sunburn. Use it every day, even in winter.

Navigation

Hikers need a good map of the area they plan to explore. Even with a map, hikers can get lost. Hikers often use the Sun to determine directions. If they walk toward the setting Sun, they know they are headed west.

The right equipment

Hikers should always carry a compass and a map and know how to use them. They need to check the compass and map frequently during the hike.

Do not panic

People who lose their way in the wild must stay calm. Groups should never split up to look for help. Staying together, close to the original route, improves the chances of an early rescue.

Never at night

Trying to walk to safety at night is not recommended. Many hikers have slipped and fallen to their deaths at night in unfamiliar areas. Being lost is scary, but being lost and hurt is much worse.

A compass and a map help hikers find the correct route.

Survival facts - Did you know?

Younger children should hug a tree if they get lost. That way, they will remain safely in one place until someone finds them. It's harder for rescuers to find somebody who keeps moving from place to place.

People who are lost should look for features, such as rivers or streams, found on a map.

TRUE STORIES

Montana territory, 1823. A bear attacked hunter Hugh Glass. He was left badly hurt and alone. It took him six months to crawl 100 miles (160 kilometers) for help.

Carry a detailed map of the area in a transparent, waterproof bag.

The compass needle always points north.

A GPS (Global Positioning System) unit pinpoints a location.

What to Wear

Weather conditions often change in a flash, so hikers should always dress in layers. Avoid cotton clothing, because if it gets sweaty or wet, it stays wet. Wet clothing next to skin quickly causes chills, which can lead to hypothermia.

Hiking boots

The best hiking boots are waterproof and lightweight. They should have rugged soles that grip the ground and should cover the ankles to help prevent sprains.

Hats

A person loses the most body heat through the top of his or her head. A hat helps prevent hypothermia. In hot weather, a hat also protects against sunburn or heatstroke — a serious condition that can cause death.

Bandana

A large square of brightly colored cloth has many uses. A hiker can use a bandana as a scarf, as face protection in windy conditions, or — when wet and tied around the neck — as a way to keep cool.

Hiking boots protect feet on rocks or forest trails.

Survival facts - Did you know?

Always "break in" a new pair of boots before a hiking trip. Sore feet and blisters can turn a dream trip into a nightmare!

Waterproof but breathable fabrics allow sweat to evaporate from the body.

TRUE STORIES

June 1992. Colby Coombs was climbing in Alaska when an avalanche killed two of his friends and severely injured Colby. He walked four days through the snow and over a glacier to safety.

Choose a "breathable" jacket that allows moisture to escape.

Wear a lightweight, waterproof jacket in warm weather.

Choose a heavier, breathable jacket for cooler weather.

A windproof, fleece jacket adds a layer of warmth.

Food and Drink

Fresh air seems to make most people eat more than they normally do when inside. Outdoor activities burn lots of energy. Hikers must remember to eat before they are hungry and drink before they are thirsty.

Drink plenty of water

Most people need 8 cups (2 liters) of water a day, and hikers should drink even more water than that. Hikers should always carry water with them.

What to eat?

Energy bars make perfect outdoor snacks. They are easy to pack and often contain the right mix of carbohydrates and proteins. Other easy-to-carry food includes bread, crackers, boiled eggs, fresh and dried fruit, nuts, and cheese. Cans of beans, meats, and fish are also good, but they are heavy to carry and require a can opener. People entering the wilderness must bring all their food with them. They cannot go grocery shopping out there!

Drinking regularly, especially in *hot weather*, helps prevent dehydration.

Survival facts - **Did you know?**

Kissing under the mistletoe is a Christmas tradition. Mistletoe is a parasitic plant, and its berries are poisonous to people and animals, including housepets.

TRUE STORIES

Bluejohn Canyon, Utah 2003. A boulder pinned Aron Ralston between canyon walls. Aron freed himself by cutting off his arm with a small knife, then walked to safety.

A hot meal tastes great outdoors. Some hikers and campers carry a lightweight backpacking stove with them.

Trail mix contains nuts, seeds, and dried fruit.

Energy bars usually contain fruit, whole grains, and protein.

Strips of dried fruit are easy to carry and make a healthy, high-energy snack.

Emergency!

Proper preparation helps prevent an emergency situation from turning into a disaster. Equipment and route planning are essential components of a wilderness trip.

Assess the situation

The first thing a lost person must do is consider these questions: Does anyone know the route he or she followed? How long before someone comes looking? What should the lost person do to prevent the situation from becoming worse? The next step to take is to stay as comfortable as possible and protect oneself from the wind, weather, and wild animals. The person might need to build a fire or a shelter.

The next step

A lost person may spend several days waiting for rescue and will need a water source. Most water must be purified before use. In desert conditions, collecting water may be more important than building a shelter. Finding food is unlikely to be a priority. Humans can survive several weeks without eating.

If possible, build a shelter in daylight and before bad weather moves in.

Survival facts - **Did you know?**

A well-known survival saying is: "You can live three minutes without air, three hours without shelter, three days without water, and three weeks without food."

Layered, breathable clothing and enough water and food help prevent hypothermia.

TRUE STORIES

Washington, 1995. A pilot crashed his private plane in a remote mountain area. He eventually died of exposure. He had left his survival kit, which could have helped him survive, in his car.

Make a simple shelter by tying string between trees. Cover it with a tarp.

For a debris shelter, lean a pole against a tree and stack branches along each side.

Cover the frame with smaller branches and leaves.

Gimme Shelter

Knowing how to build a shelter is an important survival skill. Make a simple shelter called a "lean-to" by leaning some branches at an angle against a vertical object, such as a rock wall.

In the bag

A big plastic bag makes a good raincoat or sleeping bag and conserves body heat. Rescuers can spot brightly colored plastic best. Fill a dark-colored bag with water and place in the sun to heat water.

Snow caves

People lost in the snow can dig a snow cave. The perfect size of a snow cave for one person is about 3 feet (1 meter) high, 3 feet (1 m) wide, and 6 feet (2 m) long. Any bigger, and the cave is difficult to keep warm. The cave needs an air hole in the roof. The entrance should be lower than rest of the cave. Snow caves are warmer than the icy air outside.

A snow shelter insulates against the cold. Keep it small.

Survival facts - Did you know?

Frostbite freezes the skin and turns it white, gray-yellow, or gray-blue. The body parts that freeze fastest are the toes, fingers, ears, nose, and face.

A mound of leaves provides a warm shelter. To stay warm when sleeping, campers should insulate themselves from the cold, damp ground by lining the shelter with blankets, small branches, or grass.

Build a dugout from a dry dip in the ground. Enlarge the hollow.

Place small branches or a tarp on top, but leave an opening.

Insulate the shelter with leaves and dirt.

Campfires

A campfire provides warmth and light and can signal rescuers. The campfire can also dry wet clothes, cook food, boil water to make it safe to drink, and keep wild animals at bay.

Building a fire

Always carry matches, a lighter, or a flint. Collect all the wood first. Stack the wood into a pyramid, then pile tinder – dried twigs, leaves, and pine needles – in between, and light it. Once the tinder is burning, add small pieces of dry wood. As the flames grow, add bigger pieces of wood. Build a campfire before nightfall.

Safety first

Campfires can start a forest fire. Keep the fire from spreading by building it on a patch of clear ground away from trees and bushes. Never build a fire on rocks near a river or use stones from a river bed around or in a fire. Wet rocks can explode when they heat up.

A ring of stones around the fire keep it from getting out of control.

Survival facts - Did you know?

Build a fire on wet or snow-covered ground on a base of green logs. Lay several logs next to each other, then add another layer at right angles.

TRUE STORIES

In 1994, Italian Mauro Prosperi got lost in the Sahara Desert for nine days while taking part in a marathon race. He ate bats to stay alive!

A large fire provides warmth and comfort but requires a lot of wood.

Waterproof matches are an easy way to start a campfire.

Flint and steel produces a shower of sparks for starting a fire.

A lighter burns with a steady flame. A windproof lighter works best.

Drinking in the Wild

Water in remote areas may look clean, but it is usually not safe to drink straight from rivers, lakes, or streams. Water must be boiled for several minutes to kill germs. Some hikers carry special filters or chemical tablets that make water safe to drink.

Water for life

Humans can live up to three or four weeks without food. Without water, humans die in just a few days. Well-prepared hikers, campers, and backpackers can purify dirty water several ways. They can boil it, filter it, or add chemicals to make it usable.

Sources of water

Rainwater is usually safe to drink without treating. Collect rain in pots, jars, or plastic sheets. Water can also be squeezed out of moss or cactus plants.

Cacti are a good source of water in a desert. Avoid any cacti with milky sap.

Survival facts - Did you know?

It is not good to eat snow in place of drinking water. Breaking through ice to get at flowing water provides water in larger quantities. Purify before drinking.

TRUE STORIES

Vietnam 2004. Fisherman Bui Duc Phuc
was lost at sea for fourteen days.
He survived by catching and eating a sea turtle.

Water always flows
downhill. Look for
streams in valleys.

Plants give off
water that
can be collected
for drinking.

Tie a clear
plastic bag over
a leafy part of
the plant and
seal it tight.

Water will
condense on the
bag. Use many
bags to collect
enough water.

Finding Food

Most people will never need to find their own food. Other people spend a lot of time in remote areas and need such skills. They learn how to hunt insects, frogs, and small mammals. They also learn which plants, roots, and berries are safe to eat.

Fishing

Fishing line and a few hooks are easy to carry and can help save lives if people get lost. Some people also learn how to make fish traps or catch fish in nets. Fresh fish cooks quickly over a campfire and tastes great. Fish with slimy skin should be washed off before eating.

There are no poisonous freshwater fish, although all fish, like this rainbow trout, should be cooked before eating.

Natural poisons

Unless people know exactly what they are doing, they should ever eat wild berries and mushrooms. About 95 percent of white and yellow berries are poisonous. Many wild mushrooms can kill, too.

Survival facts - Did you know?

Moonseed plants grow in the woods and have bluish-purple fruit that resembles wild grapes. They are extremely poisonous and can cause seizures and death.

Deer are tasty but difficult to catch. Like all mammals, they must be skinned, gutted, and cooked before eating.

TRUE STORIES

About ten thousand people in the United States are poisoned by eating wild mushrooms every year, mostly between July and September. Most of the poisonings involve children.

Find frogs buried in mud at the bottom of a pond. Cook frogs before eating.

Insects are nutritious and easy to find. Avoid eating hairy or brightly-colored insects.

Drop a worm into clean water. It cleans itself and can then be eaten raw.

Signaling for Help

People who are lost should make big letters in the dirt or snow with a stick, rocks, or their feet. If possible, the color of the letters should be different from the background. Rescue teams using planes or helicopters can easily spot an "SOS" signal marked on open ground. An "X" means medical aid is needed.

Catching the eye

Brightly colored plastic bags and bandanas tied to trees or posts may catch the eye of rescuers above. People who are lost can also use shiny objects to reflect light and signal an emergency. A compact disk, aluminium foil, and even the hologram from a credit card will reflect light.

Cell phones do not always work in remote areas.

Making noise

Anyone who gets lost should make a lot of noise. Use a series of whistles so that the noises sound as if humans are making them. Ground-based rescue workers searching on foot, horseback, or with dogs have more success at finding lost people than do rescue teams in the air.

Survival facts - Did you know?

A search and rescue team tries to learn as much as possible about the skills, health, and personality of the lost person to get a better idea of where to look.

Smoke flares do not last long. Flares should not be used unless the rescue team has been spotted.

TRUE STORIES

Alaska 2004. A labrador named Brick was lost in a shipwreck. People found Brick on a frozen island one month later. He used the only help signal he knew — his bark!

A whistle can be heard about 0.6 miles (1 km) away. Human voices do not that carry far.

A bright bandana spread out flat catches the eye. It can also be used as a sling.

Signal mirrors are small, but on sunny days, the flash can be seen up to 15.5 miles (25 km) away.

Brain Power

"I will never give up. I will survive." That's the way to think when lost. Survival skills help people stay alive for days, weeks, even months – but only if they keep their thinking straight. People who give up hope may die.

Stop and think

Someone who is lost is often also cold, wet, hungry, thirsty, tired, and perhaps injured. The most important thing to remember is not to panic. Prepare for a wilderness trip with the right attitude, equipment, and safety gear.

Staying alert

Survival skills come in handy in everyday life. Someone who knows he or she can cope with tough situations often develops a greater sense of self-confidence and may become a more productive or creative worker.

Nature treats everyone alike. Practical wilderness skills help people survive difficult situations.

Survival facts - Did you know?

People who are lost and hear strange noises at night should yell out as loudly as possible. Rescuers may hear the noise, and it will scare away wild animals.

TRUE STORIES

Utah, 2005. Lost children usually walk downhill. Eleven-year-old Brennan Hawkins walked uphill, over a mountain ridge, instead. Rescuers found him, tired, and hungry, after four days.

People with the right knowledge and skills can survive almost anywhere on Earth.

A waterproof, windproof bivy bag protects a sleeping bag.

Tarps can be used to help build a shelter or collect water.

A Swiss Army knife is easy to find when dropped in snow.

Types of Wilderness

Europe

North America

Much wilderness remains around the world. People rarely enter many of these places. Surviving in the wilderness requires skill – but even a little basic knowledge improves the chances of success.

Africa

South America

Rain Forest

Tundra

Asia

Australia

Forest

Grasslands

Glossary

at bay: to keep at a distance.

avalanche: a sudden and unexpected enormous amount of snow falling down a mountainside that sweeps away everything in its path.

backpackers: people who carry all their supplies on their backs as they hike through the wilderness, often spending many days in a row living out in the wild.

bivy bag: a waterproof drawstring bag that can fit over a sleeping bag and can serve as emergency shelter.

canyon: a deep gorge or ravine in mountainous territory.

compass: an instrument with a dial and a magnetized needle that points north that is used to find directions.

condense: to change from a vapor into a liquid. Condensation occurs when moisture in warmer air come into contact with a cooler surface or container.

dehydration: the lowering of body fluids to an abnormal level.

exposure: the state of being without shelter from extreme weather conditions, including heat, cold, wind, rain, or snow.

first-aid kit: emergency medical supplies used for treating mild injuries, such as cuts, scrapes, bruises, and first-degree burns.

flint: a piece of hard mineral (a type of quartz) that produces sparks when it is struck against steel; often used to start a fire.

frostbite: tissue injury, marked by color change and swelling, due to the lack of circulation to body parts — usually the toes, fingers, ears, and nose — that is caused by exposure to extreme cold.

GPS (Global Positioning System): an electronic receiver that uses satellite links to pinpoint a position anywhere in the world.

heatstroke: exhaustion, or a range of reactions such as shivering, headache or vomiting, caused by exposure to extreme heat.

hypothermia: lowering of the core body temperature below normal; caused by exposure to extreme cold; can cause death.

infamous: well-known for a bad reason.

map: a paper, plastic, or electronic plan of an area that shows recognizable features of the landscape.

parasitic: an organism that gets its food and nutrients from another living organism.

poisonous: deadly.

purify: to make clean.

remote: far from developed areas.

snow cave: a shelter made by digging a hollow in snow.

SOS (Save Our Souls): a call for help; can be sent electronically (a GPS signal), audibly (a whistle), or visually (a flare or smoke signal).

sprains: a severe twisting of a joint that tears or stretches internal tissues, which causes swelling and much pain.

sterile wipes: small pieces of tissue soaked with bacteria-killing chemicals.

sunsreen: lotions or creams that protect the skin against ultraviolet radiation from the Sun, thus helping to prevent sunburn.

Swiss Army knife: a knife featuring many different attachments, such as a screwdriver, corkscrew, or toothpick; first developed for members of the Swiss Army.

tarp: a waterproof sheet.

tinder: light, burnable materials, such as dried twigs, leaves, and pine needles, used to help get a fire going.

wilderness: an undeveloped area far from freeways, cities, and most people.

Index

airplane crashes 4, 7, 15
air 14
Andes Mountains 7
avalanches 11

bandanas 6, 10, 24, 25
berries 12, 22
bivy bags 27
blisters 10
body heat 10
boiling water 18, 20
boots 6, 10
brain power 26
breathable fabrics 11
Brick the dog 25
Bui Duc Phuc 21

cacti 20
campfires 18, 19, 22
canyons 12
cell phones 24
chocolates 7
clothing 4, 6, 10–11
    layers 10, 11
compact disks 24
compasses 6, 8, 9
condensing water 21
Coombs, Colby 11
credit cards 24

dayime hikes 6–7
debris shelters 15
deer 23
dehydration 12
deserts 14, 29
drinks (see food and drink)
dugouts 17

emergency information 6
emergency situations 14–15
energy 12, 13
energy bars 12, 13
exposure 15

first-aid kits 6, 7
fishing 22
fleece jackets 11
flints 18, 19
food and drink 4, 6, 7, 12–13, 14,
    20, 21, 22, 23
footwear 6, 10
forests 29
frogs 22, 23

frostbite 16
fuels 18

Glass, Hugh 9
Global Positioning Systems (GPS) 9
grasslands 29
groups 6, 8

hats 10
Hawkins, Brennan 27
heatstroke 10
hiking 4
hypothermia 15

ice 20
insects 22, 23
insect repellents 6

jackets 10–11
Jeracki, Bill 17

knives 4, 6, 27

"lean-to" shelters 16
lighters 6, 19

mammals 22, 23
maps 6, 8, 9, 28–29
matches 6, 18, 19
mirrors 5, 6, 25
mistletoe 12
mobile phones 24
moonseed plants 22
mountains 6, 7, 15, 29
mushrooms 22, 23

navigation 8–9
night hikes 8

parasites 12
plants 22
plastic bags 6, 16, 21, 24
pocket knives 6
poisons 22, 23
Prosperi, Mauro 19
purifying water 14, 20

rain forests 28
rainwater 20
Ralston, Aron 13
rescuers 5, 6, 8, 16, 18,
    24–25, 26, 27
roots 22

shelters 14, 15, 16, 17
shiny materials 24
shouting 24, 25, 26
signaling 5, 6, 18, 24–25
slings 25
smoke flares 25
snow
    avalanches 11
    caves 16
    eating 20
"SOS" signals 24
sprains 10
sunscreens 6, 7
Sun navigation 8
survival kits 6, 7
survival skills 4
sweating 10
Swiss Army knives 4, 27

tarps 15, 17
trail mixes 13
tree hugging 8
tundra 28

water 6, 12, 14, 18, 20–21
weather conditions 10
whistles 6, 24–25
wild animals 18, 26
wilderness 28–29
wood 18
worms, eating 23

"X" signals 24